The Creation Serie[s]
A Bible-based Readi[ng]

CW00348479

Sea Creatures

Carole Leah
and Sharon Rentta

NOTE TO PARENTS AND TEACHERS

The Creation Series consists of eight books based on the Genesis account in the Bible. This is the fourth book of this series and it has been written from a Christian viewpoint. It is intended to be read *to* 3-4 year olds. The whole series prepares children to read and extend their vocabulary. In this book children can develop and practise preparatory skills for reading as well as appreciate the greatness of God in creation.

BIBLE REFERENCES

All Bible references are in bold throughout and are as follows: p12 Genesis 1:21.

ENCOURAGE CHILDREN TO:

* Talk about the illustrations and retell the story in their own words.
* Count different kinds of sea creatures, e.g. yellow ones; round ones, fish etc.
* Draw their own sea picture with their favourite sea creatures in it.
* Memorise the Bible verse and its reference (see page 24).
* Learn the different parts of a fish from looking at a real fish - its tail, fins, eyes, mouth, scales.
* Talk about sea creatures being born e.g. whales giving birth and fish laying eggs (see pages 14-15).
* Ensure that the children know the meaning of all these words: *created* (made); *creatures* (living things that have been made and that live in water and/or land); *young* (little ones, babies).

<u>Carole Leah</u> became a Christian at a youth camp when she was seventeen years old while reading a Gideon New Testament. She felt called to write these books so that young children would learn the truth about God while also developing their reading and vocabulary skills. Several people have worked alongside Carole as she wrote this material but she would like to especially dedicate these books to the memory of her dear friend Ruth Martin who gave so much support.

All scripture quotations in this publication are from the Good News Translation in Today's English Version - Second Edition Copyright © 1992 by American Bible Society. Used by Permission.
Text copyright © Carole Leah.
Illustrations copyright © Sharon Rentta.
ISBN: 978-1-84550-532-5 Published by Christian Focus Publications, Geanies House, Fearn, Tain, Ross-shire, IV20 1TW, Scotland, U.K.
www.christianfocus.com

Todd, Joy and Daniel are in a garden.
See what they are doing in this book!

The three children are with Todd's mum.
They are looking at some fish in a pond.

Look for the crabs!

Can you find more than 10 pictures of crabs in
this book?

Did you know that crabs walk sideways?

In the beginning

no creatures lived in the sea.

God spoke and

made all kinds of sea creatures.

He created great big sea monsters.

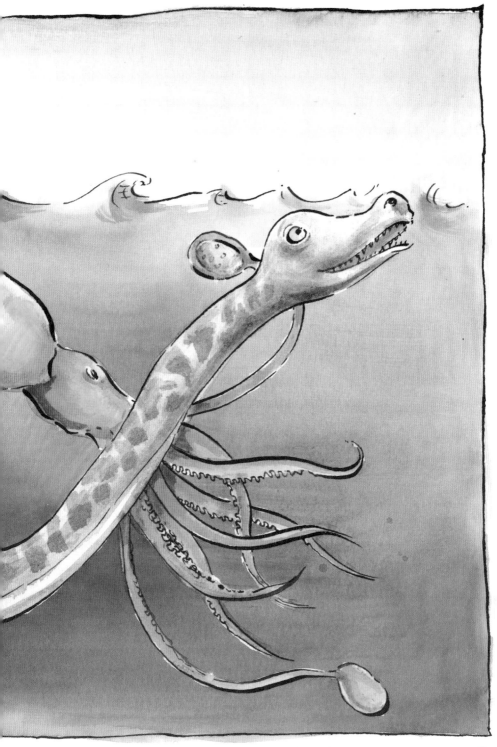

He created beautiful fish and

colourful coral.

What interesting life
God made in the sea!

God blessed all the sea creatures.

...God was pleased with what he saw.

God told the sea creatures

to have many young ones.

God told them to fill the sea.

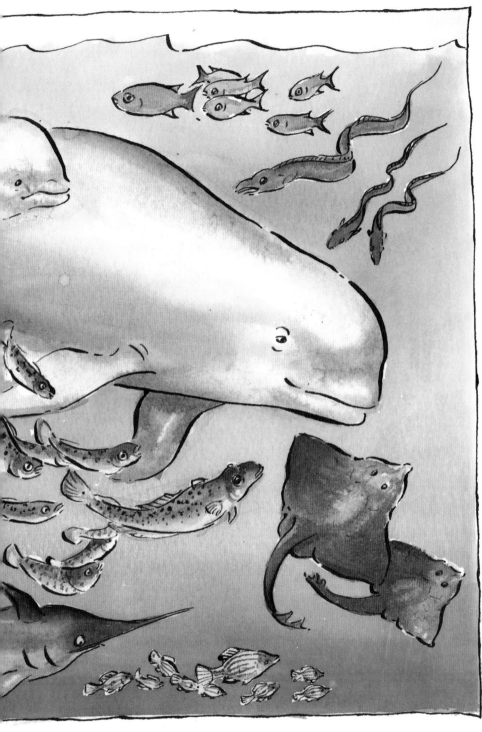

Now, Todd loves to see

the huge whales and sharks.

whales and sharks

17

Daniel loves to watch the dolphins doing their tricks.

Joy likes to see the little sea horses and wriggly eels.

EELS

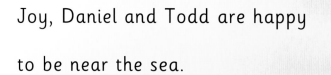

Joy, Daniel and Todd are happy

to be near the sea.

It's fun to find God's sea creatures

at the seaside!

...God created... all kinds of creatures

that live in the water...

Genesis, chapter I, verse 2I